Brinkley's tails continue . . . .

Berner Bless

Laura and

The Tails of Brinkley the Berner

Author and Art Director: Laura Leah Johnson
Illustrator: Rex Barker
Project Director: Bethany Argisle, Argisle Enterprises, Inc.
Book Designer: Albert Howell, Meta4 Productions
Editor: Jessica Brunner
Special Thanks to: Delaney Arnold and Tina Davis, Abacus Imprints

Library of Congress Cataloging-in-Publication Data

Laura Leah Johnson, 1947-
The Tails of Brinkley the Berner: Giving of the Heart / Laura Leah Johnson;
illustrated by Rex Barker.

Summary: Continue your adventures with Brinkley and Luca James as they bring love and friendship to lost animals at their local animal shelter. After hearing about animals lost in a severe flood, the special dog friends decide to help by bringing treats and listening to their stories. Through love and generosity, everyone learns the true meaning of giving from the heart.

ISBN 978-0-9793288-1-7, 0-9793288-1-0 (Hardcover)

1. Children 2. Family 3. Animals

Printed in Singapore
10 9 8 7 6 5 4 3 2 1

Photographs courtesy of JC Meadows Photography

The Tails of Brinkley the Berner

Giving of the Heart

By Laura Leah Johnson

BRINKLEY BOOKS™

Brinkley Books, Inc.
www.brinkleybooks.com

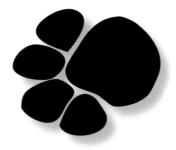
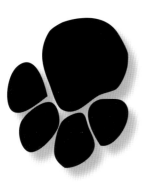

In memory of my mother
and her love
of dogs

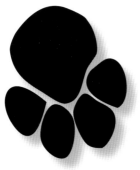
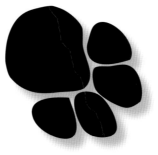

Hi, it's Brinkley and Luca! We are relaxing after our latest adventure at the local animal shelter. Read along with us and we will share with you our latest discovery.

Early each morning Momma, Daddy, and me walk down our quiet country road to get the newspaper.

It's my job to carry the newspaper back to the house.
We love to count how many jack rabbits we see along the way.

Oh Momma, Daddy, look at the headline!
Animals Lost In Severe Flooding.

How sad! I must call my best friend Luca
and tell him. He would want to know
about this.

Luca, it's Binkie. Did you see this morning's paper about the lost animals?

I saw it on TV. It makes me feel so sad. What can we do to help?

Even though we're so far away, we can help at
our local animal shelter. We can use my
allowance money to bring presents
to the animals. Let's do it!

After breakfast, we rode our bikes to our favorite store, Fideaux. Our friend, Abby, knew just the right things to buy. She chose some fun new toys and special cookies with lots of sprinkles.

On the way to the
shelter, I said to Luca,
We are very lucky. We have
our parents that love us so very
much, we have toys to play with,
healthy food to eat, and a warm bed
to sleep in.

Yes, and we share our special friendship.

Look Binkie, there they are!
Hi friends! We are here to share gifts, treats, and play some games.
Let's play ball!

Clementine the Cat sat on the fence and watched the dogs jump and play together. She smiled and purred. Clementine lives at the shelter and has an important job. She watches over the animals to make sure they are safe and secure.

When everyone was tired, we gathered around and shared the yummy cookies that Abby picked out. Then, some of the dogs began to tell their stories of how they were lost.

Topo began. I was separated from my family in a big storm.
My parents never gave up looking for me and they are coming tomorrow to
take me home. I'll miss the new friends I made here, even Clementine.

Rudi said, I didn't listen to my Momma and
Daddy, went exploring by myself, and got lost.
A kind man brought me here until my parents
come to get me. I'll never do that again.

Sarah spoke up. My parents are very old and went to a special home, but I couldn't go. I was sad but I've been adopted by a kind and gentle lady who wants to love and take care of me.

Barney barked. I don't have a new home yet. I dream about a big backyard to run and play in, a cuddly bed to sleep in, and most of all a loving family that I can love too. Don't worry, Barney, your dream will come true.

The staff takes care of us during the day and Clementine watches over us at night. She purrs so loud it's like listening to music and we all fall soundly asleep.

It was getting late and it was time for us to go home. Everyone thanked us and Abby for the toys and delicious cookies.

Clementine the Cat and the shelter manager walked us out. You made it a very special day for all the animals. Clementine the Cat meowed thank you.

Riding away, I said to Luca, Making someone else happy is the best feeling. My heart is singing! Our new project will be to find Barney a new home with a big backyard!

THE DOG IN ART VOL.IV CLARKE

THE AUTOBIOGRAPHY OF RIN TIN TIN

101 KIBBLE RECIPES

UNDERSTANDING HUMAN BEHAVIOR DR. SPOT

Call of the Wild London

Lassie

Simon

At home, Momma was excited. The news reported that the lost animals were given homes until their parents were found. That made us all happy.

When Momma was putting us to bed, she said, What you did was very special. Do you know why? We made a difference right here in town. It's important to share with those who don't have as much, and always give of the heart!

BINKIE

Remember! Give of the heart always and forever.

DEDICATIONS

To my very special Delaney, this book is for you – Brinkley

To my husband Carl with all my love – Laura

To the Berner-Garde Foundation for their work and commitment to ensure that Bernese Mountain Dogs have a long and healthy life – Laura and Brinkley

ACKNOWLEDGMENTS

My profound thanks to my brilliant team for their continued dedication and hard work: Bethany Argisle, Argisle Enterprises Inc.; Albert Howell, Meta4 Productions; Jessica Brunner, Tina Davis, Django Gurley and Robert Bergman.

A special thank you to Rex for bringing Brinkley to life in this book.

A heartfelt thanks to JC Meadows Photography for her ability to capture Brinkley in photographs.

A warm thanks to Myron for his support and always cheering me on.

MY SINCERE APPRECIATION

 Bernese Mountain Dog Clubs for their devotion and betterment to this breed.

Animal Shelters throughout the United States for their dedication to homeless and unwanted animals.

ABOUT THE AUTHOR Kindness, generosity and an unselfish heart are qualities that make Brinkley a very special dog who inspires Laura to tell his stories. He has an inherent wisdom and understanding of what's truly important in life. He owns her heart and continues to be the light of her life. Brinkley, Laura and Carl enjoy spending lazy dog-day afternoons living in Northern California.

ABOUT THE ILLUSTRATOR Rex Barker is a gifted painter who finds inspiration in the natural beauty surrounding his beachside cottage. Throughout his career, he has created hundreds of beautiful works of art that are enjoyed by children around the country. This is his first book working closely with animals. "Everything I know about dogs, I learned from Brinkley!"

Other books by Brinkley:

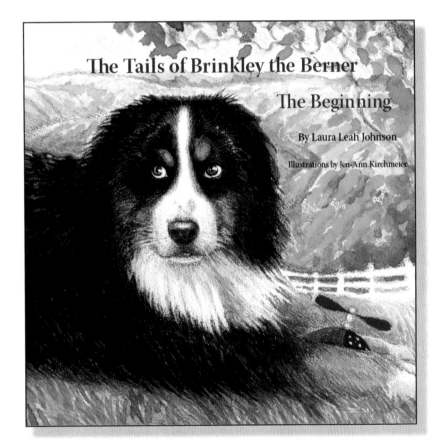

The Tails of Brinkley the Berner

The Beginning

By Laura Leah Johnson

Illustrations by Jen-Ann Kirchmeier